Surfing
The
Chaos

How to Stay Sane
in an
Insane World

Sandra Be-Taylor

INTUITIVE SOLUTIONS PRESS

Surfing the Chaos, How to Stay Sane in an Insane World

Cover Design by Sandra Be-Taylor

Graphics by Nicolette "Nixy" Rickles
Tara N. Thomson

First Edition

Library of Congress Cataloging-in-Publication Data available upon request.

ISBN 0-9777283-0-7

Sandra Be-Taylor

www.intuitivesupport.com

INTUITIVE SOLUTIONS PRESS

*This book is dedicated to
the loving memory of
Mickey Song
1940-2005*

*Your kindness and infinite compassion
for children of all ages made the
world a more beautiful place.*

Acknowledgements

Thank you to the many mentors, friends and clients that have encouraged and supported me to bring this book to fruition.

Lucia Rodriguez, Spa Director at the Ritz Carlton Resort and Spa in Maui, Hawaii, your ongoing belief in and support of my Intuitive Life Coach work has changed the lives of many grateful people.

Blair Dardik, the epitome of kindness and generosity who never said, "No." Your patience and techno wizardry is greatly appreciated.

Bruce Guttman, your many acts of quiet philanthropy make you a very special human being.

Lana Gati, you've come through for me in amazing and unexpected ways.

Andrew Molasky, your thoughtfulness and business advice is a blessing.

Sandra King, Scott Cassettari, Angelo Francois and Sarah Jane Weiss, you are my much beloved, nurturing Angels.

My daughters, Sara and Diana, you are my inspirations.

I love you all very much.

Healing is not in our heads.

Intellectual understanding
doesn't change behavior.

Chaos is the point where all that is not in balance
has stacked up so profusely that only drastic
transformation will allow equilibrium
to be restored.

All of us have experienced times when no matter
what we do or say, everything seems to fall apart.

The anxiety generated by lack of control over
our own emotional or physical environment is
terrifying in the extreme and disconcerting at best.

Victims of fierce natural catastrophes often
experience ongoing, deleterious effects of post-
traumatic stress disorder. The aftereffects of
long term emotional chaos, although conceivably
more difficult to track, are as destructive and
insidiously harmful. The negative patterns we've
developed to cope with subtle or overt dysfunction
in childhood, haunt us the rest of our adult lives.

An intellectual understanding of these events
does not modify behavior. New identity manifest
as we activate focused intention to shift
consciousness. We change ourselves, literally
reformat cellular patterning, as will is aligned
with action.

We desire Inner Peace
and
Empowerment.

What does this look like, how do we achieve this and more so, having achieved it, how do we manage to hold on to it?

How do we stay sane in an insane world?

Frances Bacon said,
"Knowledge is power."

Understanding the workings of the physical world helps us to more readily understand and function in metaphysical or emotional territory.

"So above, so below."

Just as Chaos and Order, Creation and Destruction, Light and Shadow are actually mirror images of one other, the physical and the metaphysical are two sides of the same coin.

Wholeness, perfection, is found in the union of seemingly opposites.

The Chinese yin/yang symbol, a circle divided by a wave, provides great insight. One side of the wave is black, the other white. The black half contains a white circle, the white half a black circle, ad infinitum.

It is the friction, the unfolding and enfolding wave, between apparent opposites, that creates life, movement, growth and change.

Hang in there and let's slog through some science that supports this ancient emblem as a symbol of the Dance of Life.

Iteration, the repetitive back and forth motion that is growth, suggests that stability and change are not opposites but in fact, mirror images of one another.

A number of theories in physics propose that at the smallest and presumably most basic level of matter, elementary particles generate themselves by a constant process of creation and destruction through iteration from the vacuum state.

This means that this so-called building block of nature, owes its stability not to some rocklike permanence, but to a dynamic cycling process in which the particle constantly unfolds and enfolds within its quantum field.

The cells of the human body are completely recycled or iterated every seven years. We are the same yet not the same, because we've grown and changed.

Observation of the ocean's waves provides an understanding of our own relationship to chaos and order.

With each obvious ebb and flow of the oceans surface, slight perhaps imperceptible changes also take place near the bottom of the sea. Individual waves may feed back, each into the other, and build onto themselves with ongoing intensity. This type of wave is called a soliton.

Mile after mile these soliton waves remain coupled by feedback to ultimately create a tidal wave.

The orderly system falls victim to an attracting chaos to become a chaotic system only to discover the potentiality in its interactions for an attracting order.

The soliton as a balance between the inward and outward diffusion of energy is one of the most magical phenomenon of nature.

Soliton behavior is a mirror of the dance of order and chaos.

A soliton is born on the edge. If too much energy is involved in the initial interaction, the wave breaks up into turbulence. If too little energy, the wave dissipates.

This is also true in regard to our own energy.

When we're emotionally triggered, it feels like a wave comes over us.

If we get too angry, we blow up and nothing is resolved. If we stuff our feelings, the energy dissipates and again, nothing is resolved.

Only as we embrace and surf the chaos are we able to use activated energy, creatively and constructively, to once more achieve resolution, solution and stability.

The healthiest relationships allow for open discussion of disagreements as an opportunity to create personal growth, greater depth and intimacy.

We enter into relationship with the desire for more happiness and fulfillment in our lives. The truth is,

Relationships push our buttons.

We are all familiar with the adage, "Opposites attract."

It is the interplay of opposites that motivates progress, growth and change.

The myriad interconnections of our relationships with their dynamic push/pull energetic is the dance of life.

Alternating waves of Stability and Chaos are what Life is all about.

Get used to it!

Was it Confucius that said, when something is inevitable, you might as well relax and enjoy it? I'm not sure, but what I do know is that with anything that absolutely cannot be changed, resistance only makes it worse.

Statistics tell us that oftentimes a drunk in a car wreck will walk away relatively injury free because the body was so relaxed at the time of impact.
(This is not a suggestion to
drive while intoxicated!)

It is a suggestion to learn to embrace and flow with what is occurring in present time however difficult this may seem.

Learn to Embrace the Chaos!
Make whatever is happening
in the moment, work for
your own highest good.

This requires a removal of preconception,
expectation and limited mindset.

Denial insures that our life lessons will only get more and more intense, if only as a way to get our attention. The more we resist necessary changes the more obvious and painful these challenges become.

8

We avoid escalation of negativity
as we stop to face the music.

We maximize our ability to make self loving
choices, as we look at the present with an
expanded overview, analyze real and <u>possible</u>
positives and negatives to act with forethought,
caution, wisdom and creativity.

We access and balance light and shadow with
clarity as we make observations without criticism,
judgment or attachment.

Tightly held value judgments
cloud discernment.

Events are messages.

As we become perceptive listeners, as we
hear what is said, implied and not said; we
learn, grow and ultimately protect ourselves.

Blaming one self or others keeps us trapped in
the event and does not allow us to profit from our
experiences. Looking the other way to pretend
chaos is not happening, sweeping it under the rug
to deal with it "later" or any other perambulations
that resemble avoidance only prolong the agony.

Avoidance is predicated on a lack of confidence in positive outcome.

Chaos is not going to disappear.

If one is to surf the chaos effectively it is important to become a powerful shadow dancer.

Do not be thrown off by a few missed steps or a change in the beat.

Work with the music, discern the choreography without a lot of prompting, keep moving in a positive direction and most of all...

Behave "as if" everything is going to go your way.

As you learn from every experience, mistakes are to be viewed merely as incentives to implement new and better plans.

Imagine if you will, a kitty curled up in a patch of sunlight by the window. That cat isn't going anywhere. After all, what could be better than a little snooze surrounded by warmth in the middle of the day? The sun moves away, a shadow falls, that spot is cold and, lo and behold, that kitty gets up and moves on. Remember...

It is the Shadow with its
inherent discomfort
that moves us closer
to the Light.

That's progress and just like
that kitty, growth and change
occur out of embracing and
dealing with our shadows.

What you resist, persists.

Fear of chaos will not prevent
its occurrence or help us deal
with it more effectively.

Embrace the chaos, it is
our ultimate teacher.

Chaos is the precursor to change, an integral
part of all existence. Chaos is inevitable and fear of
it only contaminates the very emotional balance
required to actually deal with it when it arrives.

Fear paralyzes our ability to see the
big picture and to operate successfully.
Fear creates anxiety and anxiety creates worry.

We worry about what's already happened, what
"would of, should of and could of" happened.

Worry dooms us to live in the past
and/or the future, completely resistant
to the present moment.

Our addiction to worry and anxiety
guarantees a dissipated life,
a life lost before it has ever been lived.

Have you ever noticed how much energy
it takes to worry? It is totally exhausting.

It takes the same amount of
energy to visualize and
magnetize a positive outcome.

Worry puts out a vibe that pulls our fears right in.

It's like this. <u>Do not think of a pink elephant.</u>

Now that you've done that,
want to put a tutu on her?

That's how worry operates.
The more we try not to worry,
the more worry magnifies and persists.

Most of us possess a deep seated resistance to change. We fear being turned loose with no recognizable signposts, no direction and nothing to hold on to.

Our comfort zone is based on the familiar even if it no longer serves us. This sounds insane but you know it's true. We attempt to avoid anything that shakes up our routine.

We're comfortable with what we know, even if it's uncomfortable!

We are put off by the Unknown
because we have no plan for it,
no rules and no precedent.

It seems a willingness to dance with shadow kicks in primarily when our shadows become more uncomfortable than our fear of change.

The outrageous amount of denial and rationalization necessary to keep the inevitable at bay, is completely debilitating.

With that kind of energy, who needs a nuclear power plant?

As we accept and celebrate

Life is an adventure of peaks and valleys

The Unknown is the Ultimate Adventure.

Our future is not engraved in stone.

Relax and Co-Create it.

14

Comforting Rules for
Dealing with the Unknown

1. Stop running.
   You'll be happily surprised at what a relief it is.

2. Turn around and face the demon.
   Check out the message in the worry,
    go to that worst place.

3. Do not resist <u>or</u> obsess on negative thought.
   Remember balance is in the consideration of
    both positive <u>and</u> negative.

4. Go to the best place.
   Visualize positive outcome.

Do not waste energy
fleeing the gift of chaos.

Take that deep breath
Stop, Look, Listen

Surrender is the antithesis to worry.

The Unknown becomes Known.
Solution and resolution can only
happen as we surrender to the chaos.

Surf the energy to create a new reality.

Go to that deepest place,
feel into your solar plexus
to access your own
personal truths.

Each of us makes the moment by moment choice to either use our fear, rage and pain creatively and constructively or be abused by it.

Chaos is the impetus that takes no prisoners.
Necessity insists we change our life.

All courage is born out of necessity.

Harness chaotic energy, use
it to fuel positive outcome.

The voice of instinct, intuition and discernment resonates through our solar plexus. Grandmothers and Wise Women through time immemorial have known, "I knew it was true because I felt it in my guts." In times of chaos it is essential to take deep calming breaths, calm and focus your energy.
Go to that deepest place, feel into your solar plexus to access your own very personal truths.

Your personal safety, your present
and future well being, is predicated
on the wisdom of your well grounded,
immediate and ongoing choices.

Allow and integrate compassion and sensitivity.
Sensitivity leads to heightened perception,
perception leads to information, information
leads to more profound resolution and solution.

Compassion allows moments of clarity
and personal forgiveness that opens us
up to our highest and best potential.

Create a game plan, do the necessary research
to commit and follow through with all that is
required to restore healthy equilibrium.

Take immediate action to reach
within as well as without
to receive comfort and assistance.

The more in tune we are, the quicker
and more immediate our access to the
instinct, intuition and discernment
that will ultimately save our lives.

Meditation is a wonderful practice to quiet
the mind. It is not necessary to sit in a full lotus
position on a hard floor, chanting some foreign
mantra over and over, in order to meditate.

Meditation is a wonderful
practice to quiet the mind.

Meditation simply requires a stillness
of our incessant internal chatter.

We achieve this silence in many ways...

A walk through a labyrinth
Sitting in our favorite chair
Watching flames dance in a fireplace
Closing our eyes to listen to our breath
Pausing to breathe the fragrance of our garden

As we practice perceptive listening
    with no agenda, nothing to say or do,
              meditation hones intuition.

Meditation allows us to be fully present in the moment with clarity and acuity.

Instinct, intuition and discernment are gifts
we are born with, gifts that protect and assure
our ongoing mental, spiritual and physical health.

These highly essential components of our
empowerment are our entitlement yet we've been
conditioned, as individuals and as a society, to
disavow our own integrity of self-knowledge.

This is clearly unacceptable.

Recognize, activate and trust your instinct, intuition and discernment to guide, inspire and protect you.

How may we trust our instinct, intuition and discernment when many of us are not even aware of their existence? How did this happen?

We are patently instructed to heed the voice of authority, be it parent, teacher, priest or government.

Our will to think on our own is broken every step of the way as we are told it is wrong, disrespectful and even punishable by law to question or defy authority.

Doubt of our own ability to choose wisely is implanted at the very root of our consciousness.

Disenfranchisement is accomplished in the most subtle and blatant of ways.

Growing up, how many of us have asked "Why?" Only to be told with exasperation, "Because, I said so, that's why."

We are admonished from earliest
childhood to give away the
power to choose for ourselves.

Our trustworthy intuitive life support systems have
become completely atrophied through disuse.

As we learn to abdicate authority
and to give up responsibility for
our own lives we are doomed to
look outside of ourselves for
security and well being.

Our very human need and desire to feel safe
motivates many of us to align with rigid
conformity or "safety in numbers."

The choice to deactivate our
own "consciousness alert systems"
renders us virtually powerless.

The price tag for giving up
the obligation to think for
ourselves is enslavement.

We become slaves to those that profit
from manipulating the masses
towards ceaseless consumerism.

We are seduced to adhere and
aspire to unrealistic and
stringent ideals of beauty.

Our value as human beings is reduced
to and measured by externals;
who we know,
career, wealth and
material possessions.

Societal as well as
individual brainwashing
has become the unfortunate
bedrock of self acceptance.

The axiom, "You can neither be too
thin or too rich." guarantees a life of
want and ongoing dissatisfaction.

We are told,
>Truth is readily accessed through ...

The intellect... The head wants to analyze,
to be seduced by statistics, to be solidly
sure through the luxury of indisputable fact...

Sentimentality... The heart just wants
to feel good, to be moved, to open up
to the saccharin purity of unbridled
yet safely choreographed emotions...

The realm of the senses...
our sexuality, well, enough said.

It is fairly obvious that in and of
themselves, these areas clearly
have their own agenda and
therefore may not be trusted.

We are encouraged to validate,
listen to and trust these very
separate parts of ourselves
because in so doing, we are
easily manipulated to buy product.

Witness the effect of the Marlboro man.
"You too can be sexy if you smoke this brand of
cigarette." Unfortunately, this much emulated male
model died from complications of lung disease.

Marketing profiteers sell us toxic products and
attitudes that if closely examined, would most
definitely be rejected as damaging to body, mind
and spirit.

To be proactive for our own highest
good, to circumvent becoming
unconscious and easily manipulated
consumers, we must learn to stay open
to self education, to access and
to trust perceptive listening.

As we learn to access, listen to and trust
our own internal gut level voice
to guide, inspire and protect us,
we are empowered to be truly free.

We are the most capable
guide to our own best life.

Choose to be Master rather than Slave.

We have the freedom to select our own
viewpoint of any event. This is called opinion.
An opinion is one persons personal truth.

The solar plexus is the one place on the
body we may trust to deliver our truth.

You may have noticed that I said "our" truth
rather than "the" truth. That's right, it gets even
more interesting from here.

Contrary to our conditioned belief in an objective truth, quantum physics refers to "truth" as "random probability."

Dr. Eugene Wigner, grandfather of wave/particle
physics, has determined,
"Energy observed through a sub atomic
microscope, may be perceived as either a wave or a
particle, completely *dependent on the observer.*"

In other words, what *you* see is what *you* get.
What you <u>perceive</u> is what you receive.

Our highly individualized perception IS our truth.

Taking this a bit further... Dr. Hugh Everret and Dr. John Archibald Wheeler's, "Many Worlds Theory of Quantum Mechanics" professes,

"The Universe is continually splitting into a stupendous number of parallel realities. In such a Universe we not only exist in an indefinite number of worlds, but all possible outcomes of any event also exists."

Many worlds exist simultaneously, therefore, Our future is not engraved in stone.

In 1960 meteorologist Edward Lorenz, Grandfather of Chaos Theory, stated that,

"One flap of a butterfly's wings in Brazil might set off a tornado in Texas months later."

Lorenz posits that, "The cumulative effect of small changes, and their timing, makes it very difficult or impossible to predict future conditions with a high degree of certainty."

What I love about all of this is, it puts *us* in the picture. We are not flotsam and jetsam randomly kicked around by an obscene Power.

We co create and define our present
and future realities by and through
our own participation, our moment
to moment choices and interactions.

Choose to co-create your reality
with focused positive intention.

I use the word co-create because I believe that
karma/past life activities or God, if you will, throws
down preordained events. How we *respond* to
these occurrences determines our situation.

A perfect example of co creation...

You're walking down the street. You see a dog.
No problem, you keep walking.

Yet, if *you've* been bit by a dog in the past, when
you see a dog, the pineal gland, in response to your
cellular memory, sends a message for adrenaline,
a liquid hormone, to suffuse your entire body.

Your heart pounds, you can't breathe, you sweat,
you smell funny and that new dog, reacting to your
terror, bites you.

Neuropeptides provide the biochemical
connection between thought and behavior.

Thoughts literally become things.
Fear turns into adrenaline.

Thoughts become matter
and effect present and future
realities without a doubt.

Cellular memory is a synthesis
of conditioning and genetics,
laid over environment and as
combined with sensory awareness
(taste, touch, smell, sight and sound)
becomes the vortex of choice.

To better manage its operation, it may be
helpful to understand the energetic of choice.

Choice is predicated on a blend of
sensory awareness and cellular memory.

This symbiotic connection is filtered through
the pineal gland, a small peanut shaped gland
located where the middle of the top of the
head and the center of the forehead intersect.

The pineal gland or third eye is where
the voices in our head like to hang out.

This outrageously intrusive inner dialogue tortures
us with doubt and recrimination. "Why did you?
Why didn't you? You should of, could of...

Aaaaah!

This vicious cacophony is the far
reaching echo of the uncertainties,
fears and accusations of our childhood.

The insistent voices embedded in our
memories circumvents our own discernment.

We are all at effect of what
I semi-facetiously call, the *unholy* trinity;
conditioning, genetics and environment.

Genetics influences sexual identity, propensities
for disease and addiction, as well as more obvious
things like eye and hair color.

After all, with all of the current prejudice in
our culture, why would anyone choose to be gay?

Have you ever noticed that some people
take one drink and cannot stop while
others easily practice social drinking?

These are all examples of genetic predisposition.

Our choice to visualize and respond in certain
ways is predicated on genetic predisposition and
exacerbated by conditioned behavior laid over the
sensory realities of our current environment.

Memory is a powerful activator and the role
of genetic memory cannot be overlooked.

Like the music formatted on a recording,
genetics and conditioning form grooves, heavily
ingrained patterns of programmed behavior.

It's time to learn how to
change the record.

Indigenous people and others who practice
earth based spirituality, ask themselves before
taking action,

"How will this action affect
the next seven generations?"

This expanded understanding is
crucial for our personal happiness
as well as planetary survival.

British biologist, Dr. James Lovelock, states in
his "Gaia Hypothesis"

"The global ecosystem sustains and regulates itself
like a biological organism. Life -- microbes, plants
and animals, constantly metabolizing matter into
energy, converting sunlight into nutrients, emitting
and absorbing gas -- clearly does more than adapt
to the Earth. The surface of the Earth is a living
body."

Life changes the Earth to its own
purposes just as we change ourselves
and one another through our ongoing
personal choices and interactions.

To make truly wise choices, it is
essential we understand, value
and respect interconnectedness
and its far reaching effect on our
individual and collective environment.

We all have intrinsic roles to play within the highly choreographed network of circumstances and appearances.

In the larger spectrum of the Universe, there is no separation between "us" and "them," there is only "we."

Huge natural disasters are very effective in bringing this obvious point home to us.

Difficult though it is to comprehend the myriad situations of our life in the moment, the overall perfection becomes apparent with hindsight.

Earth is a school.

All events are simply curriculum.

If we had nothing left to learn, we wouldn't be here.

Learn to respect and appreciate process.

The Judeo Christians say
                    "It is Gods will."

The Hindu Buddhist say,
          "You earn your present life through
              accumulated karma or actions
              performed in our former lives."

   In one we are asked to surrender to a power
much greater than ourselves and in the other,
we are encouraged to take complete and total
responsibility for our current life.

          It may serve us to interpret surrender as,
              acceptance of events rather than as an
              abdication of personal responsibility.

          It may further serve us to perceive future
              karma as motivation for right action.

   The Serenity prayer used in the Twelve Step
program is extremely useful for this type of
understanding.

"GOD, grant me the serenity to accept
the things I cannot change, the courage
to change the things I can, and the
wisdom to know the difference."

Although the crucial, life shaping combination of conditioning, environment and genetics may seem arbitrary, it is important to remember, whatever one's perspective, we still have the opportunity to co create our reality through *our response* to external and internal stimuli.

I like to perceive of God or Mother Nature as a Giant Choreographer and we as Her Dancers.

When a dance is thrown down and we have done the necessary work to be in readiness, we're Rudolf Nureyev. If we have been sitting on the couch eating potato chips, that same dance is thrown down, we fall all over our own feet.

It may not be about what actually happens but how we process and use what happens, that determines the joy in our life.

We cannot change what's already happened but we may certainly change the way we relate to it.

An agile shadow dancer uses all energies as opportunity for growth and enlightenment.

An agile Shadow Dancer uses
all energies as opportunity
for growth and enlightenment.

Take charge of your own life.

Wisdom begins as we recognize, acknowledge and activate personal responsibility for our own readiness, choices, thoughts, feelings, words and actions.

To be pro active for our own happiness
we must first make the decision to be
fully accountable for the shape of our lives.

It is time to take charge and responsibly bear the consequences of our own well thought out actions.

Our ability to comprehend and integrate external conditions coupled with a willingness to understand and take responsibility for our own participation, is the pathway to healthy choice.

Take Charge of Your Own Life

The content of our lives may seem random,
but our response to it is not.

Perceive the glass as half full
rather than half empty.

Choose to be pro active for your
own happiness, tap into and
facilitate your own highest good.

Independence and personal freedom
are by products of self reliance.

The circle is only as strong
as the sum of its parts.

Autonomy is the greatest gift we
may give ourselves and others.

Our personal integrity demands self sufficiency.

Independence allows us to
give and receive without the
prejudice of obsessive need.

We deserve the very best!

You are #1 and only <u>part</u> of your self-love
is invested in the love you share with others.

As you value and encourage
your own healthy autonomy,
as you are full unto your self,
ONLY then are you able to
share authentically with others.

Lasting and healthy relationships are created
out of mutual desire, trust, respect and
appreciation rather than obsessive need.

Do not allow regret to color your days.

Take responsibility to use
your precious energies wisely.

The basic law of physics says that energy may
not be created or destroyed, only transformed.

As this is so, the energy required for cellular
reformation is available and very alive in our
original memories.

We have a wonderful opportunity to consciously
access childhood memories, to tap into and use
their inherent energies to heal and transform
present behavior.

The healing is in the disease itself. If we do not
want to get smallpox, we vaccinate with smallpox.
If we do not want to get polio, we ingest polio.

Truths of the physical world are applicable to the
metaphysical as well. We modify our behavior as
we reclaim and transform what no longer serves us.

We go into our past for one reason
and one reason only; to access and
use the living energies of our past
(our cellular memories) to energize,
infuse and fuel our recovery.

We have no more time for whining
woundology and negative addictions.

There is no time like the
present to change your Life.

You are ONLY and TOTALLY
responsible for your own thoughts, feelings,
choices and actions as others are for theirs.

If we do not reclaim and reformat
our memories and subsequent
behaviors, we are eternally doomed
to recreate and repeat them.

Seize the day and move on!

Use the Past to Fuel a Happier Present & Future

Genetics and early conditioning are the
core of our emotional dysfunction.

Our personality is imprinted
and shaped by the expectations,
disappointments, and remembrances
of our pivotal childhood
relationships and experiences.

Patterns of behavior are formed as we
adapt to and navigate through the
day to day attitudes, conduct and treatment
of our caretakers, mom, dad, grandma et al.

As we look back through our lives
it is possible to see that many of the
protective behaviors and inherited
beliefs we assumed to survive within
our family structure have become the
very things that may prevent us from
becoming successful adults.

Our caretakers raised us to the best of their abilities, in the only way they knew how.

After all, they are at affect of their parents, who were at affect of their parents, etc.

They may very well have had the very best of intentions. That doesn't change the weight of the inherited emotional baggage we carry into our present lives.

If we do not want to be our parents and/or bequeath our damaged legacy to our own children, it is imperative we choose to recondition ourselves as soon as possible.

We have the opportunity and personal obligation to "re brainwash" ourselves. Now is the time to consciously co create our own destiny.

Our present and future happiness depends on our willingness to make different choices than our fore bearers.

It is my belief regardless of how it may seem,
our Ancestors, alive or dead, desire and support
our salvation, empowerment and inner peace.

To reclaim our memories and perceptions
of childhood is our right and is in no
way disloyal to the ones we love.

*Please remember, accepting responsibility
does not mean blame.*

To spend ones life blaming and
claiming manipulation is to become
the ultimate victim we fear becoming.

For self examination to be profitable,
it is necessary to observe our formative
years without attachment or criticism.

The blame, guilt, shame game
is a negative loop to nowhere,
serves nothing and never leads
to resolution or solution.

Cut through this boring nonsense
and agree not to play it.

To take charge of our own
present and future attitudes
and outlook is our pathway
to personal freedom and joy.

It is important to choose to see the
silver lining in every black cloud.

There are many things we may do to temporarily
assuage a negative mind set prior to and in
conjunction with cellular reformation.

Quick and Easy Fixes
to
Improve the Moment

1. Take a step back to gain a broader perspective. Figure out if what is going on is personal to you or what you are feeling is a case of "auric" infection.

The aura, best described as a psychic mood ring, may be seen through a process called Kurlian photography.

(Dr. Thelma Moss of U.C.L.A. has done major research into aura or Kurlian photography.)

The colors and intensities of our aura, invisible to the naked eye, shift and alter as our moods change.

The aura may become subtly or overtly infected by the myriad energies we come in contact with on a daily basis.

Imagine, you're in a great mood, the phone rings, you speak with a co-worker who has an attitude that has nothing to do with you, you hang up and you feel slimed. Or, you are relaxing in the living room, your partner walks in, he's in a bad mood, doesn't say anything, just sits there and you feel stressed out.

These are clear cut examples of "auric" infection.

We often waste a lot of time and energy trying to figure out what we may have done wrong or why we feel "yucky" for no apparent reason when, in reality, the negativity has absolutely nothing to do with our behavior.

To clear auric infection proceed to the next step.

2. Burn sage to purify the air.

Purifying the atmosphere in your immediate environment provides an immediate sense of lightness, calm and relaxation.

Use caution when burning sage.

Dried leaves may pop or drop creating a fire hazard.

Smudge the perimeters of the room in a clockwise direction, beginning in the east.

Smudge the telephone and other areas where negative energy may have collected.

Smudge yourself. Waft the smoke clockwise around your body, with particular attention to the bottom of the hands and feet and any other areas where you have a tendency to hold energy.

Sage is an herb that has been used by indigenous people in sweat lodge ceremonies for hundreds of years.

It is a surefire technique for clearing energy. The smoke from this medicinal plant temporarily purifies and protects the energy in your space.

If the problem is not "auric" infection and is actually something more intrinsic to your own personal condition, burning all the sage in the world won't make a bit of difference.

To temporarily neutralize your own negative emotions, it is essential to go to the next step.

3. Take a saltwater bath with candles and lavender aromatherapy.

Create a sacred environment in your bathroom. Smudge the room with sage.

Place a silver candle and a cobalt blue candle
near the tub.
If you do not have a silver candle you
may use a mirror. The metallic silver
acts as a portal for energy to be
either welcomed or released.

Light the silver candle with the words,
"I banish any and all negativity
and send it into the Light."
Light a cobalt blue candle, with the words,
"I welcome any and all energies associated
with healing, clearing, calming, and
centering, be here with me now."

Fill the bathtub with hot water.

Pour in and swirl around one third of a bag of
Alaea Sea Salt (salt laden with clay harvested from
the sacred meridians of the Hawaiian Islands.)

The intrinsic healing power of the area
of origin makes this salt, as well as
Dead Sea Salt, extremely potent.

Pour in three drops of lavender aromatherapy.
Allow the water to cool to a comfortable level
before entering and refill with hot as desired.

Soak anywhere from twelve to twenty one minutes.

Soaking in saltwater relaxes
muscle pain and temporarily
neutralizes negative emotions.

4. Cobalt Blue Visualization

Visualization is the technique whereby we
focus our thoughts to magnetize specific effects.

All colors have resonance and have major
impact on the state of our emotions.

Cobalt blue is the color most associated
with healing, calming, clearing and
centering. In China and Tibet, cobalt
blue is known as "Medicine Blue."

In the West, Vicks VapoRub and other
medicines, beauty products and designer waters
are packaged in cobalt blue containers.

The cobalt blue breath is designed to
calm focus and to enhance Inner Peace.

This relaxation technique may be done in a public
place as needed or more preferably, in the privacy
of your own home.

Close your eyes, imagine the very air
as cobalt blue in color.

Slowly breath the cobalt blue air
in through your nose

Visualize the blue air coming up to
the pineal gland, the third eye

As the blue breath reaches your third eye,
gently swirl around in a clockwise direction
and slowly blow it out the mouth.

In the nose, gently swirl
around the third eye,
blow it out the mouth.

The blue breath is performed in increments of
three unless you are native, in which case, it is
increments of four. (Different cultures access
varying integers as sacred geometry.)

Do as many increments as necessary
to better calm the strident chatter of
doubt and anxiety in your head.

This works!

The result of the cobalt blue breath
is a much clearer channel between
sensory awareness and instinct,
intuition and discernment.

Unfortunately, the blue breath and the other above
mentioned techniques provide only temporary
relief from the victimization of cellular patterning.

To assure a lifetime of pro active choice,
it is necessary to reprogram thought
patterns that no longer serve us.

Reformation of cellular memory makes a
difference in our lives only as we make a
concerted, moment by moment choice
to vitalize conscious thought renewal.

We owe it to ourselves to be
pro active; change the way we
view and operate in the world.

We do not gain confidence, grow and change by
putting our heads in the sand and hoping one day
our lives will be better.

Hope is for the hopeless.

Old responses to pain; blame, regret, self recrimination, inappropriate anger and shut down are all counter productive.

As we give away our power to choose for ourselves, repress and shut down, we quietly simmer only to inappropriately explode down the line.

Our reaction to the current event is way out of proportion, as the straw that broke the camels back is magnified through the mirror of our own repression.

Persons at effect of this massive cumulative blow up oftentimes don't know what hit them or even what they might have done to deserve it.

Stacked emotions are toxic.

It is definitely <u>not okay</u> to punish others with our problems, neither do we want to continue to punish ourselves.

Meltdowns happen as we strive to fit
into an unrealistic version of perfection.

Cultural conditioning with its programmed,
highly choreographed expectations keeps
us trapped in an inauthentic
existence of our own making.

To idealize perfection is exhausting and
creates a mind set of "not good enough"
that easily becomes a self fulfilling prophecy.

We are all light and shadow, with the very
human potential to be both saint and sinner,
feel angry or pleased, depending on
the situation we find ourselves in.

If you meet someone who denies this, run!

To be fully present in our lives, to have
real intimacy and joy in our relationships,
we must get real; be true to ourselves
and to our own genuine emotions.

We have an obligation to constructively
own and creatively work with
our own very human frailties.

It is necessary to learn new
ways to work with old pain.

If we remain trapped in and
attached to our pain, we become
our own victimizer long after the
original perpetrators have gone.

Their voices continue to rule
us as they live on in our heads.

It is imperative we go beneath the pain, access
and use the original righteous indignation inherent
in our early childhood responses (either repressed
or acted out) to fuel our healing.

Wallowing in pain keeps us ensnared
and unable to focus or energize.

A victim mentality keeps us trapped in the event
and does not allow access to the constructive
righteous indignation that will move us forward.

Remember, the basic law of physics says that energy may not be created or destroyed, it may only be transformed. The energy required for healing must come from somewhere.

Pain enervates, constructive righteous indignation empowers.

Our experiences are our own and we have every right to use them to our best advantage.

Once cellular reformation is complete, we will then own the specific tools that liberate us from the patterning of early conditioning. We will no longer be at effect of the past therefore, our family of origin no longer has the power to press our buttons.

We are finally free to love our caregivers exactly as they are.

Constructive use of righteous indignation infuses our freedom to be our own best selves.

Remember, use the energy, do not be abused by it.

Focused intention, commonly
called prayer, is a powerful and
effective use of conscious energy.

Activation of specific ceremony empowers prayer.

We mirror the knowledge that thoughts are
things as we recognize that things are thoughts.

The process of making an object a symbol
to infuse intention is called imbuing.

We more easily turn intention into action
as we symbolically imbue objects with
particular properties and significance
to ground and assist in the
visualization and activation of
our own transformative process.

Ritual transforms energy
through the symbolic.

The profound effect of Ceremony and Ritual on
the lives of millions and millions of people over
many centuries may not be overstated.

The Catholic Church may be considered a paragon of ritual. The Priest infuses water with prayer to create holy water.

A believer receives Communion and is filled with the transcendence of the Divine. The wafer is received as the body of Christ, the grape juice as the blood of Christ.

To a non believer it is merely
a wafer and grape juice.

The power of ritual transforms the entire psycho/emotional body.

What you believe is what you receive.

It is not necessary to use an intermediary for intercession.
We have the power to affect
our own transformation.

Faith, the most powerful weapon in our arsenal of healing, is enhanced through our agility and willingness to create our own sacred ceremonies, tools and symbols.

What you believe
is
what you receive.

We have the power
to
affect our own transformation.

Grounding
and
Empowerment

Create Your Own "Touch Stone"

The imbuing of a cobalt blue heart or even a simple rock creates a sacred touch stone that as handled provides instant activation of infused qualities.

Rinse the stone in saltwater.
Say either out loud or to yourself...

(Hold at solar plexus)
I imbue this stone with the power to recognize, activate and trust my own instincts, intuition and discernment to guide, inspire and protect me.

(Hold at the heart)
I imbue this stone with the power to recognize, activate and trust "ruthless compassion" or "tough love" to guide, inspire and protect me.

(Hold at "third eye")
I imbue this stone with the power to open a clear channel between my sensory awareness and my instinct, intuition and discernment to guide, inspire and protect me.

As you hold your "touch stone" you are grounded and reminded to stay true to your own best interests.

Sound as Energy Amplifier

"In the beginning is...the tone."

Singing opens us up and raises the
frequency of our energy vibration.

Voicing, toning or singing has always been part
of every spiritual practice; the cantor in the temple,
the man on the minaret, the gospel choir etc.

Toning prior to entering sacred circle opens
us up to more information, as well as
amplifies our focus and available energies.

Mother Nature is a great, non denominational,
way to visualize the Divine and in turn, brings in
more intention of support while toning.

As we tone "MAAAAAAA"
the Great Mother shows up to help
us open, amplify, ground and focus.

You may use "OM" or whatever
tone is comfortable for you.

We are in charge of our own motivation as we
co create our reality through activated intention.

Sacred Circle

Discernment and discretion are important in
all aspects of our lives. As we participate in events
that require us to open up, be seen and worked
with, (i.e., chiropractor, massage therapist, doctor
etc.) we let our guard down and are open
to any and all energies in the field or vicinity
of our process.

The conscious activation of
sacred circle provides healthy
boundaries of protection as well
as containment for activation.

All psycho/emotional/spiritual work
requires the protection of sacred circle.

Sacred circle is created through a combination
of intention and specific technique.

As necessary, Sacred Circle,
may be created silently.

Visualize spirals of clear light spinning clockwise
to create a semi permeable membrane around you.
Start at your feet and seal it at the top of your head.

How to Create a Formal Sacred Circle

1. Beginning in the East and working clockwise, smudge the area to be worked in with sage.

2. Smudge yourself (preferably after a saltwater bath) with sage.

3. Be in a relaxed position with arms, legs, ankles all uncrossed. (A crossed position blocks and reverses the energy flow.)

4. Visualize and perform the cobalt blue breath in proper increments.

5. Do your toning in the same increments as your blue breath.

6. Visualize and say out loud,
   (God, Jesus, You may use whatever name activates a feeling of safety and protection)

" Great Mother
I ask that you enclose us in your sacred circle.
Surround us with your glowing cobalt blue
spiral so that we may be completely safe
as we open up and are guided and healed
by your ineffable wisdom."

We protect and affirm our own
highest good as we reclaim our
right to design and use our own
personalized ceremonies and tools.

Ceremony and ritual augment
the transformation of the
quotidian into the miraculous.

To proceed further, we must come from a
place of personal strength and a dedicated
willingness to dance with our shadows.

Cellular reformation requires isolation of the core
experiences that shaped our previous patterning.

The healing is in the disease itself.

Grounded energy is a prerequisite
to continue the deeper work
of cellular reformation.

Do not proceed with Cellular Reformation
if you are on medication or under a
doctors care for psychological disorder.

These hyper accelerated techniques must be approached with caution and fortitude.

As in all sacred rituals, the ceremony of cellular reformation must be approached with confidence and reverence.

Early childhood conditioning continues to rule our behavior until and unless we use the inherent energy active in each memory to infuse and activate its opposite behavior.

Cellular reformation is the ultimate quantum metaphysical solution to a total and complete healing.

For aid in memory recall, technical support and to provide additional energy for grounding...

This Ceremony is best activated with the assistance of an Experienced and Trustworthy Intuitive Guide

Please read all instructions, including the Technical Guide, thoroughly before proceeding.

The Ceremony
of
Cellular Reformation
Transforms Identity

There will be two separate ceremonies,
one for the feminine, the other for the masculine.

You will require a break of at least
twenty four hours between them.

The Ritual of Cellular Reformation requires...

1. A red candle, a cobalt blue candle

2. List of hand written Original Memories
     (See Technical Support Addendum)

3. Plenty of blank lined paper and a pen.
   For ceremonial purposes, it is imperative you
   handwrite all lists before burning.

4. Matches and a large bowl for safely burning
     paper.

This work is only as effective as the
strength of your focused dedication,
commitment and follow through.

Go for it!

To Begin Ceremony of Cellular Reformation....

1. Alter the title to read,
   "I am angry with you (name) because...."
   Note the words "in pain" have been removed.

   Pain keeps energy trapped. There is
   no power in pain, only punishment.
   Constructive anger or righteous
   indignation "pops" the required
   energy to infuse your tools.

2. Cut and separate each number on your original
   list to match with its cut and separated
   affirmation tool.

3. Make an additional copy of the affirmation tools
   to be saved and used at a later date for
   integration with your second list.

4. Sage yourself and the space with sage.

5. Raise your energy by running or walking in place
   (jumping up and down, whatever) as you rapidly
   tone "Maaaaa" three times.

6. Sit down with your supplies in front of you.
   Make sure the cut up and matched pieces of
   paper will not become disorganized.

7. Create sacred circle with the words,

" Great Mother (God, Jesus, whatever name
   activates a feeling of safety and protection)
   I ask that you enclose us in your sacred circle.
   Surround us with your glowing cobalt blue
   spiral so that we may be completely safe as we
   open up to perform this ceremony of total and
   complete healing"

8. Light the cobalt blue candle,

" I call upon the Great Mother to imbue this
   cobalt blue candle with the awesome power
   of your blue, blue oceans, to clear, calm, heal
   and transform me. So it is and so it shall be."

9. Light the red candle,

"I call upon Kali, Hecate, Pele, Goddesses of
   Creation and Destruction, be here with me
   now. Imbue this red candle with the power of
   your righteous indignation so that I may finally,
   once, and for all time, own, activate and
   transform the energy of righteous indignation
   into fuel for my total and complete healing.

So it is and so it shall be."

We are now ready to activate the energy inherent in the original memory to fuel our healing.

Do not read the memory out loud until you have read it silently to yourself. To properly activate, we must get back to the intensity of our original feeling.

Take deep breaths into your solar plexus to actually feel the merited righteous indignation each individual memory evokes.

<u>If you cannot allow yourself to feel righteous indignation and you remain attached to your pain, you are not ready to do this work.</u>

10. You will read the original memory <u>one time and one time only</u>.
    Always begin with the words,
    "I am angry with you (mom or dad) because..."

    After reading, burn the memory paper in the red candle.

11. As the energy is released, immediately read
    your matching healing tool out loud,
    in increments of three,
    beginning with the words,
        "In all moments I choose to co create
            my own destiny because..."

If the first three don't fill the solar plexus, repeat
in increments until satisfied the energy has been
successfully transformed. As ready, burn the
affirmation paper in the cobalt blue candle.

You will know you have reformatted
your cellular memory by the feeling
of empowered calm suffusing
your entire solar plexus.

12. To affirm your commitment upon completion of
    clearing your entire list, repeat this sacred vow
    out loud.

" Great Mother (God, Jesus) I make a sacred
vow between myself and the Divine to do all
that I can to support my own highest good
including, diligently working with my cobalt
blueprint. By the power of three times three, so we
will it, so shall it be. So we will it, so shall it be.
So we will it, SO IT IS!"

13. Snuff out the red candle with the words,

"Hecate, Kali, Pele, Thank you for being here
with me, helping me to access and transform
righteous indignation into a total and complete
healing. I release you from the sacred circle and
know that as I require assistance to channel
righteous indignation creatively and
constructively, you are with me."

14. Snuff out the blue candle with the words,

"Great Mother (God, Jesus)
I thank you so much for being here with me.
I release you from the sacred circle and know
with every fiber of my being, you have heard
my sacred vow and will continue to support
and encourage my highest good.
Thank you and blessed be. (Amen)"

After performing the second ceremony,
we are left with two separate lists of tools.

Rest a few days before combining
the two into one to create
an integrated Cobalt Blueprint.

Cobalt Blueprint
Integration

Cobalt Blueprint Integration

1. As parents generally have similar qualities, remove duplicates.

2. Group your tools by subject.

3. Combine similar tools from each list.

4. At this point you should be left with approximately 27-45 distinctly different tools. This is manageable and very do able.

5. To create foundation and heighten effectiveness, number tools in an order that prioritizes personal safety and empowerment.

6. Tool #1 generally deals with sobriety and #2, how to constructively deal with anger. The final tool affirms your relationship with yourself and the Divine.

The title of the cobalt blueprint is,

"In all moments I <u>choose</u> to co create my own destiny because..."

The strength of your commitment will now be put into action.

1. Keep a master list for reference.
   Make copies to keep in various locations, i.e. car,
   bathroom, office. Read your tools frequently.

2. Copy each tool onto a separate and numbered
   index card. To deal more effectively with various
   situations that come up in your life isolate and
   combine pertinent tools into one card to form a
   mini/maxi tool.

Refer to and change
"homework assignments"
frequently.

3. Create a collage with appropriate images that
   evoke the essence of each tool, combine with
   easy to read tools. Post in a conspicuous place.

4. Make a recording of yourself saying each tool
   out loud, three times. Listen frequently.

Once you have created and
activated your cobalt blueprint
of accelerated consciousness tools,
there is no going back.

You now know better.

No excuses.

Vigilance and extreme dedication to your own highest good are required if you are to be effective in changing your life.

It is very easy for old patterning to reassert itself. It took many years for your original conditioning to kick in. It will take many years for your chosen re conditioning to become automatic.

Practice makes perfect. You now own the necessary tools to make healthy choices. Congratulations.

You may change your life overnight.

Be diligent in your work.

Practice Immediate Positive Thought Replacement.

Your keys to a happier, more productive and joyful life are now tangible.

You have earned your higher consciousness tools through the depth of personal experience. Use them!

Technical Support Addendum

for

Creating List of Childhood Memories

The creation of your personal list must be
done on your own and in complete privacy.

1. Follow the instructions for the saltwater bath.

   Bring a clip board with plenty of lined paper and
   a pen into the tub with you.

   To insure you <u>neutralize premature activation</u>
   of emotional energy (We will require this
   energy at a later time) prepare this list
   ONLY while in a saltwater bathtub.
   Take as many baths as you require to
   finish this list to your satisfaction.

2. Remember, <u>this work is not about blame</u>.
   It is about observation.
   Our adult selves have a tendency to forget,
   rationalize and excuse our caretakers behavior.
   To assist in excavation of early memories,
   leave your adult outside the room.
   Enter the bathtub as a child.

3. While in the tub, before and during list making,
   perform the cobalt blue breath in proper
   increments to aid in focus and relaxation.

   <u>Stay out of your head.</u>

Access your memories from your solar plexus.
Your perception of what happened is more
important than someone else's story around it.

4. Make this list using only one side of the paper.
Use as many pages as you may find necessary.
Generally there are between 25-40 issues.

5. Write one time only at the top of the list,

"I am in pain/angry (whichever verb gets the
memory) with you mom, mother
(the name you commonly used for your
female caretakers) because..."

6. Go to the next line to start numbering and
adding varying statements to the end of this
sentence. Skip a line between each number.
Make your comments short and to the point.
No essays please.

You will be making two separate
lists at two different times.

Ceremonially clear the first list
before creating the second list.
Wait at least twenty four hours
between each ceremony

One list is for dad and other
pertinent male caretakers
the other for mom and other
pertinent female caretakers.

For instance, if you were raised by a grandparent
as well as parents, you would put a "G" next to that
memory to note the correct name when doing your
ceremony.

Activation of your <u>own memory</u> provides
the necessary energy for healing.

Refer to the following list **After** you have
done your own saltwater bathtub work.

This list suggests possible wording for
creation of your own affirmation tools.

Add on, change and shape the wording to fit
your own highly individualized experiences.

It is essential your ceremonial
affirmations be hand written
for maximum efficacy.

Suggested Affirmation Guidelines

Your specific issues may be similar to those listed below.

Enclosed are suggestions for balancing, aligning and directing them accordingly.

1. Your anger hurts and scares me.

1) From this moment on, I <u>refuse</u> to shut down any longer. Intense emotions, used creatively and constructively, are vital fuel for growth and change. I do not waste the energy of my righteous indignation by denial, crying, yelling, repressing, insisting or exploding. No blame, no guilt, no recrimination.
When activated, I take deep calming breaths to source my feelings and to figure out how best to communicate in order to be better heard and understood.
As ready, I communicate calmly, clearly and effectively to create resolution and solution so that we can all feel a whole lot better.
Name it, claim it, and change it.

2. You don't accept or forgive me.

2) Wholeness/perfection is both light and shadow. I forgive myself, become wiser and stronger, as I do not overlook shadow but rather use Shadow as inspiration for growth and change. I am fine the way I am and grow finer every day as I learn from the past, live fully in the present and enjoy process rather than getting hung up in results. I forgive myself as I do my best in the moment, <u>clean it up as I go along</u> and let go of the rest.

84

3. You are an alcoholic, addict, prescription junkie.

3) I do not require substances to unleash
   inhibitions, relax and to have a good time.
   I value and maintain my healthy sobriety
   and clarity of action.

4. You are irresponsible, a blamer and a victim.

4) I have no need to blame, play victim, make
   excuses or rationalize dysfunctional
   behavior. I am ONLY and TOTALLY
   responsible for my OWN choices, thoughts,
   feelings, and actions as OTHERS ARE FOR
   THEIRS!

5. You give away your power. You're afraid to make
   your own decisions.

5) I have no need to give away my power out of fear
   of being ultimately responsible for my own
   choices. I encourage myself and others to make
   our own decisions as we are the ones who have
   to live with them. No one can make me be
   someone I am not. I value teachers and mentors
   valuable contributors to the ways in which I
   influence myself to be. I ably deal with the
   consequences of my own well thought out
   actions.

6. You are naive and refuse to look at anything that bums you out.

6) I do not hide from or ignore unpleasantness just because I don't want to deal with hassles. I proceed with intelligence and wisdom as I keep my antennae up to be aware of outside reality. "An ounce of caution is worth a pound of cure." I consciously remove my rose colored glasses to look at the big picture, both real and possible positives and negatives, to act with forethought, caution, wisdom and creativity. I think and feel into every situation before I speak, act, or sign papers.
Document, Document, Document!

7. You tell me I'm wrong and force me to do things I don't believe in.

7) I will not be made to feel guilty for listening to and honoring my own highest good. I am not a passive victim, people pleaser or a quitter. I do not take the blame for others' dysfunction nor do I accept the unacceptable. I am empowered as I speak out to protect and defend myself and my own healthy boundaries.

I am a standup individual!

8. You make me feel worthless.

8) My self love and self respect is affected by the
   way I treat myself as well as how I allow others
   to treat me. I make a fuss, say "no" as necessary,
   protect and defend my own highest good.
   My solid commitment to MYSELF affirms
   my own positive self-worth. I am worthy!

9. You abuse and ignore your health.

9) I refuse to make myself sick. I make necessary
   changes to facilitate health on every level.
   I work with a network of competent healers to
   lovingly nurture and care take my mind, body
   and spirit. My healthy boundaries and focused
   relaxation fuel my productivity.

10. You constantly worry and think the worst in
    every situation.

10) I refuse to worry and stress out about what
    I have no control over. I reclaim joy in my
    life as I surrender to the Divine and do all
    I can to co-create a wonderful life. I use my
    energy creatively and constructively for the
    highest good of myself and all concerned.
    I practice "positive thought replacement."
    to consciously create the "best case" scenario.

11. I can't trust you.

11) I only bestow love, trust and loyalty as it is
    earned through time and consistent behavior.

12. You guilt trip and manipulate me with your
    martyrdom.

12) I do not manipulate or control others through
    the power trip of guilt and self-sacrifice.
    I am not a martyr or people pleaser at my own
    detriment. I do not give myself away nor do
    I try to win love by inappropriately over giving!
    I am responsible for my own well being.
    Winning is truly taking care of my own needs
    rather than trying to get it from outside.

13. You are sarcastic, critical and judgmental.

13) My own opinion of myself is what is truly
    important to me. I am secure within my
    own beliefs, therefore, I have no need to
    prove, convince, be critical, sarcastic or
    judgmental of myself or others.

My truths may only be true
for me and that's fine.

14. You are prejudiced.

14) I see all people as unique individuals and act
    accordingly.

15. You do not know how to communicate.

15) I own my voice. I clearly, calmly and effectively
    communicate my truths with equanimity,
    without attachment, criticism or condemnation.
    I make the situation about <u>my</u> feelings rather
    than blame and castigate.
    I state my opinion and then let it go.

16. You are cold and removed.

16) I am emotionally available for myself and
    others. I give myself and deserving others
    nurturing attention. I foster healthy intimacy
    as I show up, share my feelings and create an
    environment that encourages loved ones to do
    the same.

17. You are not a good listener.

17) I am a very perceptive listener.
    I learn, grow and protect myself as
    I perceive what is said, implied, and not said.

18. You don't protect me.

18) I am not a victim. I do not tolerate trespass and disrespect on any level. I recognize, protect and defend my own (and dependents) healthy boundaries with strength and focused determination.

I am proactive for my own protection.

19. You don't trust your instincts.

19) I recognize, activate and trust my own instincts, intuition and discernment to guide, inspire and protect me. I take deep breaths to calm my emotions and to get past the voices in my head so that I may clearly integrate my solar plexus understanding.

20. You are confrontational and argumentative.

20) I accept conflict, the dance of light and shadow, as the sand in the oyster that ultimately creates the pearl of great wisdom and resolution.

A healthy discussion is not an argument.

21. You have no integrity.

21) My integrity speaks for itself. I keep my
    agreements or change them in advance
    as mutually understood.

22. You are a know it all who really doesn't know
    anything.

22) I have no need to pretend. I know what I know
    and what I don't know. I know where and how
    to get the information I require to protect my
    own highest good. I am respected as I am true
    to myself and others.

23. You play favorites.

23) I am subtle in my favoritism. I treat people the
    way I would wish to be treated.

24. Your humor is sarcastic and cruel.

24) I am not passive-aggressive nor do I hide
    negative feelings behind cruel humor.
    I am not sarcastic at the expense of people's
    feelings. My humor unites rather than puts
    people down.

25. You don't make time for me.

25) I do not just pay lip service. I prioritize my
    relationship with myself, family and good
    friends. I make time to smell the flowers.
    I authentically show care in thought, word and
    action. You cannot "make it up" down the line.
    I delight in sharing.
         People I care about, know it.

26. My needs are not important to you. I can't
    depend on you.

26) I consciously make the time and effort to tune
    in, be compassionate, respectful, sensitive and
    responsive to my own and loved ones feelings,
    needs and desires. I am dependable and may be
    counted on to be fair and just, warm,
    nurturing, kind, gracious and generous
    because it makes me feel good to be that way.
         When I love, you know it.

27. You punish me for asking questions.

27) I value learning and intelligence in all its
    myriad forms. My healthy curiosity is a lovely
    gift that inspires me to learn and grow.
    I acknowledge and encourage my own innate
    brilliance. I ask questions to protect my own
    highest good.

28. You are needy and co dependent.

28) I create healthy, strong and lasting relationships out of <u>mutual</u> trust, respect, desire, and appreciation rather than obsessive need. I value and maintain my own healthy autonomy and do not give away this freedom under any circumstances.

   I take care of myself on every level.

29. You are jealous and competitive.

29) I have no need to be jealous. I am pleased with my own (and others') many gifts, skills and abilities. I view competition as healthy inspiration rather than destructive put down. We are all winners as we acknowledge there is more than enough good for all of us.

30. You don't praise or encourage me

30) I generously share praise, inspiration and encouragement with <u>myself</u> and others.

   It feels great to say, "You did good."

31. You are stressed, unhappy and won't do anything to change it.

31) I view discomfort as a beacon of enlightenment that direct me to areas where I am resisting understanding.

I more fully navigate my personal success, grow braver and stronger everyday, as I honor, listen to, confront and redirect negative energy towards positive solutions.

I am ultimately more at peace as I face shadows head on (without avoidance) and process through to solution.

Resolution is the ultimate in relaxation.

32. You are narcissistic. You always think everything is about you.

32) I do not personalize. We are all the center of our own universe and act accordingly.

We are also interconnected.

I look at many sides of a situation to moderate my actions and to be more responsible for my own conclusions.

33. You always compare me to others and I come out short.

33) We are all unique therefore incomparable. I am more than enough. I love my self exactly as I am with no need to prove or convince.

34. You are a hypocrite.

34) I encourage moral integrity as I teach through positive example.

35. You make me feel I don't deserve to have.

35) Abundance is my birthright. I enjoy and access abundance through grace, right livelihood, delight in my chosen field, fortitude and ability to make life-affirming choices and changes.
I am rich right now!

36. You are ashamed of our heritage.

36) I do not forget who I am. I acknowledge, appreciate and share my history, as appropriate.

I honor my culture and ancestors with respect and reverence.

37. You are a control freak.

37) To control means to be responsible for.
   I am only responsible for me and that, in itself,
   is a full time job. I don't tell people how to run
   their lives. I am secure and confident as I
   surrender my need to control each and every
   moment and situation.
   My spirituality empowers me to
                    Let go and let God.
          True power is in my <u>knowing</u> and
          <u>fully believing</u> I am "protected."

38. You think sex is shameful.

38) My sexuality is sacred and fun. My love for
   myself and partner sets me free to express my
   most giving and passionate nature.
   My sensuality is a delight.

39. You don't think before you speak.

39) I do not blurt! I am personally, politically,
   professionally and socially astute.

40. You betray my trust.

40) I respect my own and others privacy and
   confidentiality. I am trustworthy.

41. You give yourself away and tell everyone everything.

41) Knowledge is power. I am circumspect in my communication. I am discerning about who I share my deepest truths and feelings with.
I am protected as I share information ONLY on a "need to know" basis. It is not necessary to share everything with everyone.

42. You are passive/aggressive.

42) I am honest with myself (and others) as I admit and courageously communicate issues head on, admit rather than blame or punish in underhanded, passive/aggressive ways.

43. You don't value your own needs and desires.

43) I'm not running a popularity contest!
I refuse to go into denial, do other people's dirty work, be manipulated, ripped off, play martyr, or people please at my own detriment.
I satisfy myself and maintain personal integrity as I only do, give and share what pleases me.
I am number one, and only as I prioritize my own needs am I able to share authentically with others.

44. You never make time for fun and spontaneity.

44) I live a happy and healthy life as I take
    calculated risks to be more spontaneous in
    the moment. I am fun! I enjoy life.

45. You hold grudges.

45) I forgive myself and others for things I cannot
    change. I neutralize resentment and
    defensiveness as I take responsibility for my
    own participation and point of view.
        Holding grudges only hurts me.

46. You abuse your power.

46) I have earned my power and influence and am
    very astute in the ways I use it.
    I do not pressure myself (or others.)
    I make a positive difference in my own and
    others' lives. I contribute only as it is in the
    highest good to do so.

47. You have no gratitude or appreciation.

47) I co create a more fulfilling life as I learn from
    the past and live fully in the present
    with gratitude and appreciation.
        All of life is precious.

48. You are phony.

48) I do not play "lets pretend" just to make my life
    "easier." My personal integrity demands I am
    true to myself and others.

    Only as I am authentic with myself and others,
    allow and process all emotions, both light and
    shadow, will I experience true and ongoing
    happiness.

           To be diplomatically authentic
              is to be ultimately kind.

49. You are not generous with yourself or others.

49) I share generously ONLY as there is mutual
    respect and appreciation or with all
    expectations clearly stated, understood and
    mutually agreeable. A closed fist can
    neither give nor receive! I allow myself to
    receive (as well as to give) with joy.

50. You are demanding.

50) I facilitate opportunity for healthy exchanges
    as I do not make demands but rather
    encourage, enlist and inspire to create what
    I desire.

51. You have unrealistic expectations.

51) Expectations (from myself or others) only lead
   to pressure and disappointment.
   I value encouragement and inspiration over
   demanding expectation.

52. You put things off and never finish what you
   start.

52) I value, acknowledge and integrate the wisdom
   of my maturity, have more fun, relax
   to enjoy the fruits of my labor, as I step up to
   the plate to handle my commitments and
   responsibilities in a timely and responsible
   manner. I live my dreams and make them
   realities as I proceed with loving dedication
   and focused determination, one step at a time.

53. You act like a child and expect others to take
   care of you.

53) I refuse to be treated like a child or to give
   away my power on any level. Financial
   independence is essential for freedom of choice.

   My autonomy allows me to be free to be
   generous to myself and deserving others.

54. You are impatient.

54) I work to be compassionate, forgiving and
    patient with myself and others. I enjoy
    the process as I stay in present time.

    It's about the ride, not the destination.

55. You are a complainer.

55) I do not waste energy by whining and
    complaining nor do I need to win the "who had
    the worse day" award. Whining consumes too
    much energy. I give myself a tiny window for
    complaints and then, get down to the business
    of solutions. I use my energies creatively and
    constructively.
    Just get it done, shoulder to the wheel
    and move on.

56. You are superficial.

56) I consciously take the time and effort to look
    beneath the obvious to perceive what is
    true for me. I value my integrity above
    materiality, substance over surface.
    Money does not ensure happiness.
    I enjoy material things for what they are
    without losing sight of what is truly
    important.

57. You are a gossip.

57) Idle chatter, gossip and partying are not the way I choose to define my life.

Where one puts ones focus, says everything about who they are.

I am a person of great substance and worth.

58. You put me in the middle between you and my other parent.

58) I calmly, firmly and clearly refuse to be drawn into battles that are not my own.

I won't take sides, be a go between, dumping ground or mouthpiece nor do I encourage or expect others to speak for me.

It's important for the appropriate people to work it out between themselves.

59. You are not gracious.

59) "To receive is wonderful and to give is Divine." I am fulfilled through my care and generosity. I am gracious to myself, my family, friends and community.

60. You live in the past.

60) My mortality is inspiration to fully appreciate
the Now. I let go of the past as I
acknowledge opportunities, lessons and
potentials in the present. I continue to learn,
grow and improve my life. I am in gratitude
and appreciation for my health, well being and
every joyous moment.

61. You don't know how to say "no."

61) I look at the overall context to determine the
ultimate highest good for all concerned.
I say "no" as necessary. I believe in the value and
importance of healthy limitations to provide
and build valuable context for a productive life.

62. You are not warm and affectionate.

62) I am demonstrative, warm and affectionate
within healthy boundaries of mutual trust,
respect, desire and appreciation.

63. You don't make our house a home.

63) I value, create and maintain inner and outer
harmony. My environment inspires me to
relax, achieve and create.
My home is sanctuary.

64. You pout and punish me for things I don't even know I did.

64). In some cases, silence is <u>not</u> golden.
I (and others) have a right to our feelings.
The more one represses, the worse things can get when they finally surface.

People are not mind readers. I work to understand and to clarify my feelings, to analyze and to intuit the most positive ways to communicate so that I may be more readily understood and possibly have my needs met.

65. You are blinded and manipulated by your sexuality.

65) I am aware that my powerful sexual urges may have a tendency to blind me to possible negative consequences. I will not be manipulated or controlled by my sexuality.

I make healthy choices to be intimate only with those who respect, care and are sensitive to <u>my</u> highest good. To ensure lasting satisfaction and happiness in relationship, I consciously work to align my sexuality with love and nurturing emotions.
I protect myself as I practice safe sex.

66. You are a hypochondriac.

66) I do not get sick or align with negativity as a
way to get attention. I give myself the
attention I require to support my own highest
good. I value & lovingly nurture my body,
mind and spirit.

67. You are closed minded

67) I learn and grow as I listen to the feelings and
opinions of others to make my own well
thought out choices. I am open to change as
I integrate what makes sense to me.

68. You are a workaholic.

68) I enjoy my life as I maintain a healthy balance
of work and play. I generously, willingly and
consciously share quality time and positive
attention with myself and loved ones.

You cannot "make it up" down the line.

69. You don't apologize when you are wrong.

69) I apologize and make amends as necessary for
the mutual highest good.

70. You take your problems out on me.

70) I handle negativity in a clear and direct fashion, <u>as it comes up</u>, therefore I have no need to "kick the dog." I do not accept the unacceptable. If I don't like something, I find a way to change it, leave it or make it work.

71. You always settle for second best.

71) I compromise ONLY as it is in my total, highest good to do so. I realize that there is a price tag to everything and to try to get something for nothing is a disservice to all involved. I do not give myself away nor do I ask others to do so. I own my integrity and that can't be violated. I willingly and generously pay for quality.

72. You assume rather than check things out for yourself.

72) To ass/u/me makes an ass of you and me. No excuses. I communicate clear, direct agreements in a totally responsible fashion. I dot my i's and cross my t's.
I am responsible for my own well being, proactive for my own protection.

73. You base your happiness on what other people think of you.

73) I do not live my life to please others. If you externalize value, you will be constantly striving and never attaining. I live my life in service to the Divine. My own approval of myself and my relationship with the Divine is all that is truly sacred to me.
      "Be still and know I am God."

74. You are a gambler and don't care about the well being of your family.

74) I am fiscally responsible. Money is a form of energy. I use energy wisely, creatively and constructively. I enjoy money as a good time ONLY as I am able to provide for my own (and dependents) comfort and security without undue stress.

75. You are always trying to change me.

75) I know when and how to leave "well-enough" alone. It is not my job to make people over. I accept people for who they are with no expectation of change.
We all do what we believe to be right for ourselves and live with the consequences.

76. You are a liar.

76) To lie, takes too much effort. It's easier to live
with myself as I don't worry about getting
caught. The truth liberates me from guilt
and sets me free to be fully myself.
Honesty with discernment is the best policy.
To leave out painful information, is not a lie!

77. You can't take a compliment.

77) I am open, allowing and encouraging in my
willingness to receive. I know how great it
feels to give, therefore, I allow others to
experience that with me. I am worthy of
nurturing, generosity and compliments!
I deserve the very best.

78. You ignore me.

78) My personal universe is more peaceful as I do
not invite negativity through insensitivity.

I do not ignore people in a room with me.

I am very aware of how my words and actions
may affect myself and those around me.
I access and promote caring words and
actions. I make amends as appropriate.

79. You don't value your talents.

79) My talents are a gift from the Divine. I do not
hide behind poor scheduling or false modesty
as a way to underplay and undermine my
commitment and devotion to my own
mission. I dedicate time, energy and focus
to encourage my talents to bloom.

80. You do not let yourself be known.

80) Modesty and privacy are respectful as long
as they are sincere. I do not shut down my
relationship with myself and others out of
"false" modesty based in self judgment,
criticism and fear.
I create depth and intimacy, encourage
relationship, am open and sensitive to
the mutual highest good, as I communicate
personal history in self loving, constructive
and considerate ways.
I am respectful to myself and others as
I allow intimacy only in healthy increments.

81. You make everything complicated.

81) Difficult does not equal better. I more readily
access solutions and enjoy life more,
as I simplify and cut to the bottom line.

82. You have no compassion or acceptance.

82) I am empowered by my compassion for myself
and others. We are all a work in
progress. I accept and forgive as I learn
and grow from all experience.
    "Love me, love my shadows."

83. Your constant need for attention embarrasses
me.

83) I have no need to exaggerate, be flashy or overly
aggressive to get attention. My very being
speaks for itself. I promote my talents with
highly effective subtlety.

84. You make me wear clothes I hate.

84) I have great taste. I dress to please myself.
I appreciate, nurture and maintain my
creativity and personal sense of style on
every level.

85. You are a compulsive neat freak.

85) I appreciate cleanliness and order with no need
to be fanatical. I am comfortable in my own
home.

86. You are an enabler.

86) I encourage self sufficiency by allowing
others to honor and make clear decisions
for themselves. I am supportive only as
appropriate and appreciated.
To enable is to be responsible for.
I am only responsible for me.

87. You are erratic.

87) I am not dictated to or controlled by impulse.
I choose to intelligently respond rather than
spontaneously react. I think things through.

88. You are selfish.

88) We are all selves therefore "self" ish. I am not
naive nor do I blame myself (or others) for
trying to manipulate situations to go our way.
Only as I prioritize and meet my own needs
am I able to authentically share with others.

89. You over commit and under perform.

89) I protect my own highest good as I take on
responsibilities and commitments only as I am
able to complete them with ease and
competency.

90. You don't love me unconditionally.

90) I am never alone. I am eternally protected,
nurtured and loved unconditionally by
MY SELF and the Divine.

These affirmations provide a template
for adaptation and creation of specific
tools to redress our own unique
childhood experiences.

Edit and Use
them appropriately.

Be specific
and
Creative.

Remember,
Words are powerful.

Congratulations.

You may change your life overnight.

Be diligent in your work.

Practice Immediate Positive
Thought Replacement.

Your keys to a happier, more productive
and joyful life are now tangible.

You have earned your higher consciousness
tools through the depth of personal experience.

Use them!

www.ingramcontent.com/pod-product-compliance
Lightning Source LLC
Chambersburg PA
CBHW030148310326
41914CB00086B/40